SHAKESPEARE MEMORIAL THEATRE

[from a drawing by Ronald Searle]

GLEN BYAM SHAW, C.B.E.

DIRECTOR OF THE SHAKESPEARE MEMORIAL THEATRE
FROM 1952 TO 1956 JOINTLY WITH ANTHONY QUAYLE,
FROM 1957 TO 1959 ALONE

Shakespeare
Memorial Theatre
1957-1959

A Photographic Record
with an Introduction by Ivor Brown and
Photographs by Angus McBean

MAX REINHARDT
LONDON

The publishers acknowledge with thanks the help they have received in the production of
this book from the management of the Shakespeare Memorial Theatre,
especially from John Goodwin.
All photographs are by Angus McBean, with the exception of the following numbers:
Roger Wood: 88–91, 94–98
Camera Press Ltd: 92 and 93
Tony Armstrong Jones: 99–104, 106–107

Introduction by Ivor Brown

1957

The plays selected for 1957 were nicely representative of Shakespeare's full reach. For comedy there were 'As You Like It' and 'The Tempest', for the Romans 'Julius Cæsar', for the English chronicles 'King John', and for English pre-history and romance 'Cymbeline'.

We began in Arden. Glen Byam Shaw's production of 'As You Like It', decorated by Motley, moved most happily from 'winter and rough weather' to the hey-ding-a-ding of Arden's spring and summer. On the first night Peggy Ashcroft was under handicap of a sore throat, but her Rosalind defeated all signs of impediment. One of the best tributes came from Derek Granger, the percipient critic of the *Financial Times*, who wrote, 'The shades of fancy and of wonder which cross her face at the moment of her falling in love are as sweetly defined as the light and shower of April weather'. She had an Orlando of fine looks, carriage, and speech in Richard Johnson, and together they made one of the most familiar of the comedies seem new and spontaneous as the forest lovers went their ways of devotion and of wit. There are always cross-currents of opinion at Stratford, and some critics were slightly reminiscent of Jacques in their willingness to suck melancholy out of this spring-song. But the general verdict was voiced by W. A. Darlington in the *Daily Telegraph*: 'I cannot call to mind a production of "As You Like It" that has charmed me more.'

The supporting parts had much praise and deservedly so. I enjoyed especially the ability of Robert Harris to persuade me that I had never previously been informed that 'All the world's a stage'. It could be said that this Jaques was insufficiently crabbed and sour, but there are two ways of reading the part. It is possible that Jaques was acting and enjoying a misanthropy which he did not wholly feel and it was this kind of forest recluse, more mellow at heart than he cared to admit, that Robert Harris so well realised. It is difficult for Celia to make her impact when there is a Rosalind of the first lustre, but Jane Wenham was well able to do so, while Patrick Wymark proved that Touchstone can be much better company than he sometimes seems. This production fully merited the honour of being visited by Her Majesty the Queen on June 14th.

Douglas Seale's grasp of the Histories was manifest in the season's second offering, 'King John', and so was the command of colour always shown by Audrey Cruddas. Alec Clunes brought a jovial energy and the right rasp of angry humour to the part of the Bastard and

Robert Harris gave us all the high temper and low dealings of a monarch who defined both France and Rome and then, ready to be a murderer and to challenge his own barons, went down in baffled fury and bodily pains. With Joan Miller to speak the rages and despairs of Queen Constance, there was ample utterance of a text in which Shakespeare was pouring out the full eloquence of martial poetry as well as voicing with an ample virulence the personal ambitions and their tragical frustrations.

A word might be said here of the company as a whole. It has been too easily assumed of late that Shakespeare at Stratford depended on its stars. But Glen Byam Shaw, while enlisting starry support, had always seen to it that the company had substantial strength in its middle ranges, a strength without which the excellence at the summit might have been wasted. The work done in the years which this volume covers by Cyril Luckham, Mark Dignam, and Anthony Nicholls, to mention only three of the supporters, revealed a triumvirate of most commendable ability. In this case the first two of these were King of France and Papal Legate; they showed their constant capacity to create a vivid character. King John himself is so vehement in his antagonisms that he must have metal worthy of his attack. Such opposition was notably provided, not only by the gusty Bastard played by Clunes but by the enemies abroad.

Glen Byam Shaw's direction of 'Julius Cæsar' showed his familiar concentration on the purpose of the play and his disinclination to be diverted by the lure of unnecessary innovation or display. From Motley's soaring Roman pillars the drama of conspirators and crowds moved effectively to the tented field. The three leading parts of Brutus, Cassio, and Antony were taken by Alec Clunes, Geoffrey Keen, and Richard Johnson. This offered a severe challenge to all three, for in no case was there any type-casting. To move from the earthy, lusty Bastard in 'King John' to be the pensive Brutus and 'Noblest Roman of them all' is no easy journey, and Clunes seemed to wear the toga less easily than the accoutrements of the Anglo-French wars. The Cassius of Geoffrey Keen was handicapped in the minds of many by memories of Sir John Gielgud in this role both in film and play; the mingled chagrin and petulance of the conspirator, who had more commonsense and less ethical integrity than his colleague, were not quite driven home by the player on this occasion, perhaps because his many successes on the screen had mitigated his theatrical attack. Mr Johnson, so happy as a young lover in Arden, found Antony's mature vehemance less easy to propel. All three performances were, needless to say, up to a high Stratford standard; but the Stratford summit was not fully climbed. Cyril Luckham, however, coped admirably with the usually intractable part of Julius Cæsar; the declining invalid was there and so were the remains of greatness. Mark Dignam was no less helpful as Casca.

And so to ancient Britain. For Peter Hall's production of 'Cymbeline' Lila de Nobili provided a setting appropriate to the strangeness of a play in which the Renaissance rubs shoulders with the primitive. Blended Gothic and Italian styles were apt to a piece in which courtiers and cave-dwellers, early British and Roman soldiers, must commingle. Peggy Ashcroft's Imogen was faithful to the exquisite qualities of a part whose writing has evoked the loftiest of tributes from the literary critics. Fidelity was in her being and courage was most tenderly breathed. When Imogen took to her boy's attire for the journey into wildest Wales she might have been more attractively attired; the play is essentially romantic and there is no need for a close realism of the tramping life. Her Posthumus was bravely carried out by Richard Johnson and there was a vividly odious Cloten provided by Clive Revill who was later to show his versatility by admirable clowning as Trinculo in 'The Tempest'. Geoffrey Keen's Iachimo was a determined, if not lurid, villain, and took the difficulties of the bedroom scene and its trunk-emergence with skill and with success. Robert Harris coped vigorously with the title-part. The play had more justly been called 'Imogen' since, at least to the modern audience, it is her sweet spirit that brings intermittent sublimity to a play where barbarism is laced with beauty. Memory lingers on her lines and on her who spoke them.

Last venture of the year was 'The Tempest' with Peter Brook not only producing but decorating and arranging the music. The lovers of tradition had some shocks to take; the songs of Ariel had their lyric loveliness subdued and old harmonies were missing. The settings were hardly complimentary to the island scenery and the vegetation was described by one critic as providing 'a proper obstacle race of hanging fronds'. The masque could be accused of in-adequacy in spectacle. Yet there were tremendous qualities visible. Sir John Gielgud brought an intensity of realism to his Prospero whom it was utterly impossible to confuse with the tedious and verbose magician that he sometimes seems. Instead we met an angry middle-aged man, a displaced V.I.P. now nursing a most genuine grievance and moving with com-pulsive humanity as well as irate energy from his revenge to his pardoning.

Alec Clunes's Caliban was an atrocious monster in aspect. Yet how critics differ! One found him 'an obscene spectacle'; another was reminded of Barrie's dog Nana in 'Peter Pan'. The latter judgment was presumably reached in consideration of this Caliban's ownership of a heart somewhat human beneath a most inhuman hide.

The clowning was uninhibited and Patrick Wymark, with the Trinculo already praised, gave us a rich show of neatly contrived 'business'. With a Robeyan look and something of a bowler-hat on his head this Stephano leered, growled, and went toping to the top of foolery's in-vention. The production in an improved form was later taken from Stratford to Drury Lane where during the Christmas holidays it drew an enormous and well-satisfied public.

1958

The opening of the season of 1958 was made with 'Romeo and Juliet'. Glen Byam Shaw, with Motley as decorator, directed. In 1954 he had shown his excellent capacity to set the tale of heated blood and clannish hate coursing along the sun-baked streets of combative Verona, while the moon-lit night evoked the gentler passions of the star-crossed lovers and the lyric note that fills this tragedy with an irresistible harmony of sound amid the unharmonious snarlings of the rival factions.

There was one early mistake soon remedied. The costume and make-up of Richard Johnson's Romeo handicapped him. He was condemned to look more like an out-of-work actor than the scion of a lordly family at large in a world of Elizabethan foppishness. For some reason not easy to discern, Romeo, though a long and famous role, is rarely rewarding to the actor. People perhaps expect too much and few players of reputation emerge with their names enhanced. But Mr Johnson's performance had virtues of speech and a compelling authenticity of feeling.

Dorothy Tutin's Juliet made an admirable start. Here were the rapt girlhood and the bewildered ecstasy of extreme youth. It is a common-place that an actress who can be perfect in the early Juliet may lack the histrionic stamina for the later episodes which demand such range of power. On the first night the performance, after its exquisite start, became uneven: some passages failed to carry their full pathos, others could in no way be criticised. One could sense the first-night strain and its stiffening effect upon work that would soon be relaxed and gain in confident expression. This did occur. Her performance at the end of the season showed that Miss Tutin had gained greatly by her Stratford experience.

It was good to have Angela Baddeley as the Nurse, providing her racy portrayal of that good prop of the Capulet establishment, whose heads, played by Mark Dignam and Rachel Kempson, were real people and not just familiar names. Edward Woodward's Mercutio promised well for his roles to come in the company he had recently joined. Anthony Nicholls doubled Chorus and Prince in a fine-sounding way and there was the right humanity in Cyril Luckham's Friar Laurence. The season's opening night was one to justify high expectation. Here, surely, was a team that would settle down to make the year one of balanced and satisfying achievement.

My chief and a most vivid recollection of 'Twelfth Night' is of the delightful partnership of Dorothy Tutin and Geraldine McEwan as Viola and Olivia. Olivia has sometimes seemed to be a colourless role, all loveliness and no life. As played by Miss McEwan the lady, though not long bereaved by the death of her father and a brother, had made a good recovery from grief and had by no means lost her sense of humour. Indeed Olivia had as much mischief as of mourning in her composition. She was now a smiling beauty who could derive her own amusement from Orsino and his embassage. Beside her Miss Tutin made a most youthful and appealing Viola. In their passages together they made one fancy that they were boy-players of the Elizabethan stage; one could also believe that, if the two boys who played the parts for the Lord Chamberlain's Men in 1601 were as well-graced and entertaining as these two, Shakespeare had every reason to be satisfied.

Michael Meacham brought good looks and good delivery to the part of Orsino. Dr Hotson has maintained that this part was written to honour a visiting Italian grandee of that name. Therefore it should be given high quality of performance. In any case, it is a more important role than is sometimes apparent; Mr Meacham, a newcomer to Stratford, made good play with his opportunity. Sir Toby was naturally safe in the hands of Patrick Wymark who, while able to go all out for absurdity, knows that in clowning, especially in Sir Toby's part, some modesty of nature must be observed. Since Hamlet followed closely on 'Twelfth Night' it may be that his rebuke of over-clowning, in his talk with the Players, was consequent upon some excessive foolery on the part of his Illyrian drolls. Shakespeare could have no quarrel with the pleasant fooling of this Sir Toby and with the Aguecheek of Richard Johnson which was well in tune. Malvolio gave Mark Dignam his richest part of the season and his command of the dry and haughty manner showed him at his best. Cyril Luckham made an older man of Feste than is usual, and justified the innovation.

The scenery and costumes by Lila de Nobili took us on an Adriatic journey with plenty to take and hold the eye. Peter Hall's production was a happy one and not marred by any determination to impose strikingly new notions on a masterpiece which can be left to run its own course among the music of love and the canakin's clink. The medley of revel and romance was established with beauty sufficiently surrounding.

The producer of Shakespeare at Stratford has always to face one dilemma. His public is a double one. Small, but vocal, is that section which, knowing Shakespeare and theatrical practice intimately, wants novelty of approach and favours experiment even to the verge of the fantastic. The much larger public, with no pretensions to specialist knowledge, wants to see the play: if there are stars in the sky, so much the better. But a clear statement of the author's purpose is what most meets their need. One can always rely on Glen Byam Shaw to appreciate that reasonable demand and to meet it with fidelity to the text. Fantastication is justifiable where the play is one of those not usually given, one which, either through excess of horrors, as in 'Titus Andronicus', or through some absence of the master's hand, as in 'Pericles', needs tactful concealment by directive invention. But 'Hamlet' does not ask for titivation or for the ingenuity that elaborates new readings. It is its tremendous self and Glen Byam Shaw, knowing that the play is here most certainly the thing and that far the greater number of Stratford's play-goers come to 'Hamlet' for 'Hamlet's' essence and not for an exhibition of a producer's personality, gave us a rendering with nothing to distract and nothing to impede the simple and rapt attention to the text.

Certain things were notably well done. The Play Scene was most impressively mimed and acted and Hamlet's address to the Players was so naturally, so lightly, so amusingly taken by Michael Redgrave that one seemed to be hearing it there in Elsinore and not as part of a familiar experience. Mr Redgrave was capitally fresh and fascinating in the prose passages; the wit in banter and repartee came across in a most lively fashion. To emphasise this is not to detract from the urgency of the poetical declamation and the considered delivery of the soliloquies. But I shall remember this 'Hamlet' especially for his aptness in argument, his teasing humour, and his likable humanity. The self-pity was played down: there was full suffering, of course, but my general impression was of a Prince of nimble mind and tongue, a credit to the University of Wittenberg as well as the poignant voice of a vexed conscience and a tortured spirit. The uglier side of Hamlet, at least for modern taste, was smoothed over. The callousness of 'I'll lug the guts into the neighbour room' was omitted.

The setting, by Motley, was columnar and starkly simple. The scarlet uniforms of the Royal Guard blazed and the sounds of a revelling court came floating aptly to the battlements. Seeing 'Hamlet' late in the season, I surmised that Mark Dignam's King had lost some sap in the intervening period. He was more acid in reproof of the Prince than 'bloat' in the relish of luxury. Googie Withers as the Queen gave us a foolish, bewildered beauty, a soft-hearted sinner, very different from the sharp-witted woman presented by Diana Churchill in 1956. Dorothy Tutin's Ophelia, no symptoms of derangement spared, was intensely moving, a girl sinking in turbid waves of distress before the last immersion in the willowy stream. The Polonius of Cyril Luckham was excellent, being a credible Chamberlain, no dotard but a crusty and tetchy as well as a loquacious official. For the Ghost, not a dug-up corpse but a powerful

[11]

and human visitation, Anthony Nicholls spoke finely. In all there was a forthright, unaffected delivery of a text given at length as well as with simplicity.

The year's 'rarity' play was the semi-Shakespearian 'Pericles', which certainly carries ample evidence of the master's hand in its second half but, before that, makes a somewhat tedious cruise through the Near East with no aid of major poetry to fill its sails. That it can be produced simply and with fair results was proved by Douglas Seale at the Birmingham Playhouse a few years ago. But the great resources of the Stratford stage and the greater public to be served obviously demanded a more spectacular method. Here is, in the main, a second-rate piece which asks for first-rate disguise to cover its weaker portions.

Tony Richardson determined that the most effective remedy was to have us all at sea. The stage was set by Loudon Sainthill in marine fashion; episodes on what Cleopatra called 'the varying shore o' the world' were set within a frame of shipping. The Chorus, an important part since the plot needs plenty of explanation, was given by the author to a very early English poet, John Gower, whose tomb, incidentally, is in the mother-church of the Elizabethan theatre, now Southwark Cathedral, where Shakespeare's brother, Edmund the actor, is buried. The role was assigned, for no reason I could appreciate, to a coloured actor, Edric Connor, who sang or intoned the lines in the guise of a sea-captain – or a bo'sun at least. The words, so necessary for exposition, were somewhat obscured by this musical delivery, which was a handicap to those perplexed by the goings-on.

Mr Sainthill's costumes richly established a note of romantic savagery and it seemed to be forgotten that Asia Minor was the early home of the highly civilised philosophy and poetry for which ancient Greece was famous. It could, however, be replied that the author (or authors) of the play cared nothing for this and that the tale abounds in bestial crimes and brothel-squalour. So the dark, barbaric aspect could be well justified. The storms at sea – this is a far more tempestuous play than 'The Tempest' – were well realised with swinging ropes and tottering mariners. The audiences could hardly be expected to admire the play itself; but they were given ample chance to enjoy it as an occasion for nautical alarums and for an imposing assemblage of potentates on land with their cohorts of infantry. It is frequently said of a minor player that 'he carried a spear'. Rarely have there been more, and more formidable, spears to carry.

The Mytilene brothel-scenes were presented, without flinching, on a stage rising from below decks. So it could fairly be claimed that the piece launched by Wilkins – at least that is the usual guess – and rescued from ship-wreck by Shakespeare, was given every aid of productive technique. In the midst of monarchs, mariners, pikemen, and brothel-keepers, Richard Johnson plodded bravely on through the life and hard times of Pericles himself. When the drama moved from all a-board to all-a-bawdy, Angela Baddeley was properly improper and luridly 'a proper sight' as the hostess of a 'night spot' in Lesbos which had obviously never heard of its world-famous poetess Sappho and was resolutely heterosexual in its pleasures. Stephanie Bidmead as the Lady from the Sea and Rachel Kempson as a murderous queen contributed effectively to the strange medley of romance and 'tough stuff'; Geraldine McEwan's Marina was a pretty innocent abroad.

It was a pity that the production of 'Much Ado About Nothing' by Douglas Seale with scenery by Tanya Moiseiwitsch (assisted by Ellen Meyer), costumes by Motley, and music by

Christopher Whelen, came late in August, last in the list of 1958. For it was an enchanting affair. One indignant lady, it is true, asked for her money back. What on earth was this? Shakespeare waltzing. Messina in the blues and reds of nineteenth century uniform? Was not this flat sacrilege? But the public in general were ready to welcome with rapture the fanciful invasion of another century and this presentation would have packed the house throughout the season. (Not that there was any difficulty about packing the house with any of the plays, even 'Pericles'.) The early Victorian costumes were accepted not only as a delight to the eye but as a proper companion to the hey-nonny spirit of the play. Pauline Grant's direction of the dances was an additional pleasure and the final piece of design with Benedick and Beatrice deserted by the light-foot company and treading their measure alone made an exquisite curtain.

Michael Redgrave and Googie Withers were most happily matched in the early battle of wit-crackers and the later marriage of true minds. They took the beautifully fashioned prose of the dialogue in easy, conversational style; sometimes I thought that they were over-casual in their resolution to be natural. How often, especially in 'Much Ado', did Shakespeare write a line that merits a 'throw-away' technique? But that is a small criticism of a joint performance large in elegance and élan. Geraldine McEwan had been admirably suited and successful in her playful rendering of Viola in 'Twelfth Night': some of the tricks of voice had lingered, less suitably in her Hero. I had the misfortune to miss Cyril Luckham's Leonato, which I was told was characteristically amusing: Donald Layne-Smith proved a capital understudy. Richard Johnson contrived to cover up the unlikeliness of Don John's monstrous and inhuman cruelty and Anthony Nicholls was an impressively Victorian Prince of Arragon in the full fig of the period.

Comic invention was fresh and gay. The concealment of Benedick, when he is being gulled with talk of Beatrice's love, was neat. He was lying on cushions behind a gigantic sun-shade. Patrick Wymark's Dogberry, in uniform, a Napoleon of the rag-tag Watch, was as rich a piece of fooling as one expects that admirable droll to provide. One has known occasions when the verbal glitter and high jinks of this comedy have been made the matter of a laboured gaiety, while the 'hey-nonny' spirit overflowed. There was no such error this time. The Victorian period forbade excessive Tudor-costume flourishes and offered instead an invitation to the waltz for which Pauline Grant and Christopher Whelen had set the pattern and the melody.

At the close of the 1958 season the Shakespeare Memorial Theatre company were able to accept, with the encouragement and help of the British Council, an invitation to play in Russia for four weeks, visiting Leningrad and Moscow. Long and complicated arrangements were finally settled. A large party of players, stage staff, and management, though missing their Christmas and New Year holidays at home, gladly undertook the journey and the undertaking was most happy in its results.

The productions carried were those of 'Hamlet', 'Romeo and Juliet' and 'Twelfth Night', a heavy commitment for all concerned. The social reception by the British Ambassador as well as by the Russian artists was of the warmest and most generous kind. As far as their work in the theatre allowed, the playgoers could have been engaged in party-going and sight-seeing without cease, but some rationing of the lavish hospitality had to be made if the prime object of the visit was to be properly achieved and Shakespeare's plays given the freshest possible performance.

[13]

Michael Redgrave added to his labours of the player those of a welcome lecturer and all who had time to do so were able and glad to accept invitations to visit the Russian theatres.

There could be no doubt that the Russian artists of the theatre as well as general audiences were deeply impressed by the strength, speed, and beauty of our English productions as well as by the individual skill in performance. The students in Leningrad, where all seats had been booked, were admitted to a dress rehearsal and offered such prolonged applause that the players had never known anything like it. Reception in Moscow too, where all seats for all performances were sold within forty-eight hours of the opening of the booking, was no less cordial and complimentary. It was considered by those in charge that some of the finest work of the Stratford year was done by the company in those final and very strenuous weeks in Russia. Dorothy Tutin's Juliet, for example, was now at its peak of achievement, having gained greatly in power since its opening at Stratford in the spring. Particular credit was also due to the stage staff who had to cope with unfamiliar stages and conditions and had to take over the very important task of lighting the plays with apparatus new to them and with a very short time in which to do so. The visit may have been slow in the arranging: it was immediate and immense in its success.

1959

The year of the Hundredth Season, honoured by a cluster of great names in the cast, opened on April 7th, 1959, with 'Othello'. Tony Richardson produced. The early emphasis was on speed and still more speed. There was only one interval and that was reasonably taken after the ending of the Turkish war and the cashiering of Cassio. The early flurries, alarms, revelling, and fighting were presented with the utmost vigour and skill in crowd-manipulation. Stormy weather at Cyprus was of hurricane strength; the drinking-scene was a party indeed.

It is impossible to have such concentration on furious action without some damage to the text. Cutting is inevitable in so long a play and Mr Richardson was not afraid to cut both here and later on. After the interval and with the goading of Othello by Iago the pace was properly reduced. Paul Robeson went through the Moor's tortures and passed on to his fury with full use of his powerful bass voice; the authenticity of his emotions was obvious and compelling. But some critics seized on a lack of response to the beauty of his words. It is commonly said of Macbeth that Shakespeare made him a great poet as well as a great soldier and the same is true of Othello. It is a severe challenge to any actor that he should be true at once to the savagery of Othello's final behaviour and to the loveliness of his words. It was plainly the opinion of the audience that Mr Robeson had not failed to meet any of the actor's problems, for the applause at the end was prolonged and tumultuous.

It would be difficult for any actress to stand up on natural terms with an Othello so dominant in physique and vocal power. Mary Ure is slight of figure and her voice seemed dwarfed amid the tempest of jealousy. But she sang the Willow Song beautifully. There was much and just acclaim of Angela Baddeley's Emilia, a dark and lusty character who might well have been wife to Iago. She avoided the refinement sometimes seen in this role. Zoe Caldwell's Bianca was a vividly plaintive trollop and Peter Woodthorpe's Roderigo a plausible 'snipe' and not another Aguecheek.

Sam Wanamaker's Iago was a scoundrel unconcealed and it was difficult to see how such a slim, insinuating scoundrel could ever have impressed the world as honest. He was at best when he was taking the audience into his evil confidence; then, as a villain frank and gleeful in his villainy, he carried full conviction. Two American accents in the leading roles were less disconcerting than one expected. Paul Robeson's thunders were little localised in intonation and one began to accept a gangster Iago, since usage has accustomed us in film and television to transatlantic tones in the utterance of a crook's intentions.

Loudon Sainthill's settings were plainly designed to symbolise the darkness of the story. He did not make things easy for the players by setting Othello's bed-chamber as an upper-room far above the ordinary stage. The great, concluding speeches were delivered under handicap of remoteness: but the audience evidently felt no sense of hampering alienation. As was said, the reception was remarkable in its warmth and generosity, even for the opening of another Stratford year, when long plaudits are a custom.

The second production was that of 'All's Well That Ends Well' by Tyrone Guthrie. Rarely performed for three centuries, this piece has come into more favour (or less disfavour) lately. When romance ruled in the theatre and it was deemed the business of woman to be womanly, the character of Helena, who insists on choosing her own husband and pursues the reluctant Bertram till she captures him, was plainly distasteful. But when the equality of the sexes, in wooing as in voting, was accepted and when Bernard Shaw had discovered Helena to be a good Ibsenite and the play a 'noble' one, the story could be valued afresh and the piece has now been given at Stratford twice in five years. Dr Guthrie believes that Helena is one of the best of Shakespeare's heroines and he proved his affection by directing the piece sympathetically for her and with a wise choice of a boyish-looking Bertram (Edward de Souza) who was too young and too callow to know what he was missing. The selection of Zoe Caldwell, a newcomer of the year before who had distinguished herself in small parts, to play the all-important role of Helena was well justified. The girl was so resolute to win because she truly adored. The performance was rich in young, ecstatic love and the pains of its frustration.

It could be deemed odd that a play seemingly so anti-romantic and anti-Victorian should, like 'Much Ado About Nothing' in the previous year, be set in Victorian uniforms. But the experiment, decorated by Tanya Moiseiwitsch, turned out happily. We began in a Roussillon whose park had an air of Anouilh's excursions into old French châteaux, and there was Dame Edith Evans to be enchantingly the Countess, most gracious of Shakespearian mothers. Then there was the Court of France with its young officers clicking their spurred heels in an imperial manner round the invalid and later restored King (Robert Hardy). Parolles, played by the versatile Cyril Luckham as a very modern mixture of cad, sponge, and blusterer, went to the wars with Bertram, and the wars were apparently in an African desert. Whatever their location, they were highly diverting campaigns. On the first night an enraptured and television-addicted schoolboy could be heard announcing with rapture 'It's The Army Game'. (Bernard Bresslaw would not have been out of place in the platoon.) It was good to hear boyhood so delightedly discovering that Shakespeare need not be a schoolroom taskmaster.

Such gaieties showed the Guthrie touch in their humorous contrivance and few, if any, felt that the Bard was having his beard impolitely pulled in his home-town. For the essential story of Helena's love was not overwhelmed by the comedy business, which is certainly not Shake-speare's best and needs some added intervention to give pleasure now. To remind us of the play's better qualities there was Dame Edith, with her beautiful delivery of the Countess's lines, accompanied by a perfect courtier in Lafeu (Anthony Nicholls) and relieved of Lavache, the Clown. Since this supposed droll is not one of Shakespeare's better jesters – though Edward Atienza's rendering in 1955 did finely for him – one had to be a strict purist to lament the cutting of him. Altogether Dr Guthrie had confirmed his view that Helena and her story, whether she is dancing a pavane or a waltz, are too good to be permitted further absence from Shakespearian revivals.

Peter Hall directed 'A Midsummer Night's Dream' as a wedding revel in a lordly Tudor home. There is very little doubt that the play was originally written for such an occasion. Therefore the direction was historically correct in purpose and it is highly probable that the fairies were first played by boys not girls. It is also quite certain that Mendelssohn was not there to supply the now almost inevitable score. So nobody could question the authenticity of the production as a journey in search of origins.

Such a presentation meant of course that those expecting a bevy of little girls on tip-toe and pirouettes to nineteenth century music were disappointed. It also meant a confused kind of scene since the lordly home had to sprout some boskage if there was to be any kind of forest. Mr Hall and his designer Lila de Nobili might have been so far austere as to cut the boskage altogether and leave the woods to the words. Indeed, the permanent setting, a wooden bridge that formed the balustrade of the hall, remained throughout. Yet by ingenious lighting we had the woods too when needed, a beautifully swift transformation from house to glade. Even so, the Stratford audiences were given very much what the milord commanded on a wedding-night in the fifteen-nineties.

There was one charming lullaby by Raymond Leppard and otherwise less reliance on the appeal to ear, far more on the appeal to laughter. The frantic lovers were given free rein to be absurd. Priscilla Morgan's dumpy, petulant Hermia and Vanessa Redgrave's lanky, lachry-mose Helena were great fun. The Duke's lines were beautifully spoken by Anthony Nicholls beside his warrior queen (Stephanie Bidmead) who, though buskined, did not, as text suggests, bounce and was more of a charmer than a battle-cruiser of the ancient Amazonian kind.

The clowns were led by Charles Laughton, his white hair browned off for the occasion. This Bottom was a large and bemused and by no means 'bully' in the modern sense. He loomed and bulged at the centre of things, without being the tyrant of the mummings. The demise of Pyramus, so loth to perish, was vastly amusing. Peter Woodthrope was a properly masculine Thisbe. Ian Holm's Puck was a pert piece of mischief, more of the street than of the forest. Robert Hardy gave character as well as cadence to the lines of the angry Oberon and Mary Ure's Titania was clearly delivered as well as a delight to the eye. No production of 'The Dream' can ever satisfy all demands. Soothe the romantics and you annoy the Tudor realists. Peter Hall took that risk and, while depriving playgoers of traditional pleasures, achieved what he intended.

Peter Hall's direction, with the settings by Boris Aronson and costumes by Riette Sturge Moore, gave 'Coriolanus' a barbaric, not a conventionally Roman background. This stressed the correct date (490 B.C. instead of 49 B.C.) of the proud soldier's triumphs and disasters and turned the road to the Forum into no classic avenue but a sinister street where savagery was natural. The battle-scenes were brilliantly tumultuous and the physical side of the acting, which culminated in Sir Laurence Olivier's breath-taking death-dive, provided a wonderful display of lunging and leaping. But there was far more to the performance than athletic abandon.

Sir Laurence made the anti-proletarian speeches flash like gleaming metal: at the same time he mitigated the arrogance of Coriolanus with an infusion of ironic wit that was enchanting. Possibly Shakespeare did not intend the hero turned traitor to have quite so much personal charm; this Caius Marcius could hardly have been so much hated. But there was such subtle turning of a line and such perfection of phrasing and timing that here was a rendering never to be forgotten. And here too was a magnificent Roman matron, fire-breathing at first and later most poignant in humiliation. Dame Edith Evans gave us the heart as well as the hauteur of Volumnia, while Mary Ure, as the tacit Virgilia, lived up to her husband's praise of looks and manner as 'my gracious silence'.

The mediating counsel of Menenius was delivered with a searching and humorous sagacity by Harry Andrews and the Tribunes were vividly presented by Peter Woodthorpe as a gruff type and by Robert Hardy as a slick and oily master of intrigue. For the Volscians Anthony Nicholls, accustomed to the meritorious roles, had now a chance to be a vessel of venom and his vibrant delivery of hatred's eloquence rang in the ears as Caius Marcius rolled at his feet. In this production crowd-clamour and sword-play, character-acting and declamation, mingled to win new honour for a tragedy unduly neglected in its own time and after.

'King Lear', in August, ended the Hundredth Season. It also ended the directorate of Glen Byam Shaw, who, first with Anthony Quayle and later in sole authority, had been in charge of Stratford productions since 1952. During his eight years he not only engaged the theatre's greatest players to act at Stratford, but also arranged four London seasons, sent tours overseas to thirteen countries and produced twelve plays himself – a most exacting as well as triumphant achievement. Throughout he had been endeared to all who worked with him because he knew his job, knew his people, and handled both with the expertness of a skilled professional and with the comprehension of an understanding and sympathetic personality. But there comes a tide in the affairs of artists and 'Glen', feeling its urge, decided that it was time to seek another sea-coast of Bohemia. And it was he himself who suggested to the Governors that they appoint as his successor the brilliant Peter Hall, only twenty-eight, whose work was already well-known at Stratford. Patrick Donnell, continuing as Assistant to the Director, makes – with his mature experience of Stratford's problems – an admirable link between 'Glen' and Peter Hall.

Like all the outgoing Director's productions, this 'Lear' was vigorous, lucid, and scrupulously fair to the play and the players. I cannot remember a production in which the ravelled sleave of the plot was better and more clearly handled. Thus all the parts, of which some are often unsatisfying, had their chance to satisfy and did. Cordelia was no insipid Miss, but emerged firm and memorable in the person of Zoe Caldwell, with Stephanie Bidmead and Angela Baddeley presenting no less firm a front of she-devilry as the heartless sisters. An Edmund more subtle and less wolvish than most and a most original Edgar were added by

Robert Hardy and Albert Finney, while the appearances of Ian Holm, Cyril Luckham, and Anthony Nicholls as the Fool, Gloucester, and Kent were guarantees of distinctive support. The Motley decoration had ingenious severity and some notably bright moments, especially when we moved to the sea-side. The storm was left to the poetry: the stage-management was not encouraged to add to this compulsive verbal torrent the 'dreadful pudder o'er our heads' of stage-machinery.

The occasion was, in the eyes of the Press, Charles Laughton's, but not in the eyes of that great actor whose Lear was essentially in the play and never rampaging all over it. Here, as most critics agreed, was a comparatively gentle Lear, a crumbling figure from the start, not violently conscious of lost authority but gradually making a piteous acquaintance with his own folly. As the cruelties were massed over his head, Laughton, not at his best in the storm scene, moved on to a muted majesty of pathos. The madness on the cliff was played with a heart-rending medley of reason and unreason, of the crazy fancy and the cutting line. Those who had missed the early flash of a conventionally choleric Lear now met the full tragedy of the foolish and the fond old man. It was a performance that grew in pressure throughout the evening and the calm of the finale was more breath-taking than any agony amid the wind and the rain.

August, 1959.

THE PLAYS

1957

STRATFORD
As You Like It [1–8]   *King John* [9–14]
Julius Cæsar [15–20]   *Cymbeline* [21–27]

STRATFORD AND LONDON
The Tempest [28–34]

THE CONTINENT AND LONDON
Titus Andronicus [35–38]
[1955 production]

1958

STRATFORD AND RUSSIA
Romeo and Juliet [39–49]
Twelfth Night [50–57]   *Hamlet* [58–66]

STRATFORD
Pericles [67–77]   *Much Ado About Nothing* [78–87]
Russian visit [88–98]

1959

STRATFORD
Othello [99–107]
All's Well that Ends Well [108–117]
A Midsummer Night's Dream [118–126]
Coriolanus [127–134]   *King Lear* [135–141]

1. Orlando [Act III, Scene 2]
Neither rhyme nor reason can express how much

1957
AS YOU LIKE IT

Orlando, *Richard Johnson*
Adam, *James Wellman*
Dennis, *Derek Mayhew*
Oliver, *Robin Lloyd*
Charles [the Wrestler], *Ron Haddrick*
Celia, *Jane Wenham*
Rosalind, *Peggy Ashcroft*
Touchstone, *Patrick Wymark*
Le Beau, *Peter Cellier*
Duke Frederick, *Mark Dignam*
The Banished Duke, *Cyril Luckham*
Amiens, *Rex Robinson*
First Lord, *Antony Brown*
Second Lord, *Peter Palmer*
First Page, *Peter Whitmarsh*
Second Page, *Michael Saunders*
Corin, *Donald Eccles*
Silvius, *Robert Arnold*
Jaques, *Robert Harris*
Audrey, *Stephanie Bidmead*
Sir Oliver Martext, *Donald Layne-Smith*
Phebe, *Doreen Aris*
William, *Toby Robertson*
Hymen, *Gordon Wright*
Jaques de Boys, *John Murray Scott*

Lords, Ladies, Attendants and Foresters:
Molly Tapper, Mavis Edwards, Elizabeth Evans,
Pamela Taylor, Thane Bettany, Barry Warren,
Edward Caddick, Simon Carter, John Davidson,
Henry Davies, William Elmhirst, Kenneth Gilbert,
Julian Glover, John Grayson, Norman Miller,
John Salway, Gordon Souter, Roy Spencer,
Christopher Bond

Directed by GLEN BYAM SHAW
Scenery and costumes by MOTLEY
Music by CLIFTON PARKER
Dance arranged by PAULINE GRANT
Wrestling match arranged by CHARLES ALEXIS
Lighting by PETER STREULI

2. Orlando [Act III, Scene 2]
Hang there, my verse, in witness of my love

3. Rosalind [Act III, Scene 2]
Let no face be kept in mind
But the fair of Rosalinde

4. Le Beau [Act I, Scene 2]
He cannot speak, my lord

5. Orlando [Act I, Scene I]
I am no villain; I am the youngest son of Sir Rowland de Boys

6. Patrick Wymark as Touchstone,
Stephanie Bidmead as Audrey

7. Robert Harris as Jaques

8. Silvius [Act III, Scene 5]
. . . Then shall you know the wounds invisible
That love's keen arrows make

9. *Alec Clunes as Faulconbridge, Robert Harris as King John*

1957
KING JOHN

King John, *Robert Harris*
Chatillon [ambassador from France], *Peter Cellier*
Queen Elinor [mother to King John], *Molly Tapper*
The Earl of Essex, *Antony Brown*
Philip [the Bastard], *Alec Clunes*
Robert Faulconbridge
    [his half-brother], *James Wellman*
Lady Faulconbridge, *Stephanie Bidmead*
Gurney [servant to Lady Faulconbridge], *Rex Robinson*
Lewis the Dauphin, *Barry Warren*
Arthur [Duke of Bretagne,
    nephew to the King], *Christopher Bond*
Lymoges [Duke of Austria], *Clive Revill*
Constance [mother to Arthur], *Joan Miller*
King Philip of France, *Cyril Luckham*
Blanch of Spain [niece to King John], *Doreen Aris*
A Citizen of Angiers, *Patrick Wymark*
A French Herald, *Thane Bettany*
An English Herald, *Peter Palmer*
The Earl of Salisbury, *Donald Eccles*
Cardinal Pandulph [the Pope's Legate], *Mark Dignam*
Hubert, *Ron Haddrick*
A Gaoler, *Julian Glover*
The Earl of Pembroke, *Robin Lloyd*
A Messenger, *Derek Mayhew*
Peter of Pomfret [a prophet], *William Elmhirst*
The Lord Bigot, *Donald Layne-Smith*
Melun [a French lord], *Toby Robertson*
A French Soldier, *John Murray Scott*
Prince Henry [son to the King], *Gordon Wright*

Citizens of Angiers, Soldiers, Monks, Nuns, Servants
and others: *Mavis Edwards, Elizabeth Evans,
Pamela Taylor, Robert Arnold, Edward Caddick,
Simon Carter, John Davidson, Henry Davies,
Kenneth Gilbert, John Grayson, Norman Miller,
John Salway, Gordon Souter, Roy Spencer,
Michael Saunders*

Directed by DOUGLAS SEALE
Scenery and costumes by AUDREY CRUDDAS
Music by CHRISTOPHER WHELEN
Fights arranged by BERNARD HEPTON
Lighting by PETER STREULI

10. Pandulph [Act V, Scene 1]
                    . . . Take again
From this my hand, as holding of the Pope
Your sovereign greatness and authority

11. *King Philip [Act II, Scene 1]*
. . . young princes, close your hands

12. *Hubert [Act IV, Scene 1]*
. . . None, but to lose your eyes

13. *Joan Miller as Constance*

14. *Molly Tapper as Queen Elinor*

15. *Cæsar [Act III, Scene 1]*
Et tu, Brute ? Then fall, Cæsar!

16. *Clive Revill as*
Octavius Cæsar

17. *Joan Miller*
as Portia

1957

JULIUS CÆSAR

Flavius and Marullus [Tribunes], *Peter Cellier*
   and Patrick Wymark
Citizens, *Antony Brown, Peter Palmer,*
   Rex Robinson and Julian Glover
Julius Cæsar, *Cyril Luckham*
Calpurnia [his wife], *Jane Wenham*
A Soothsayer, *Norman Miller*
Mark Antony, *Richard Johnson*
Brutus, *Alec Clunes*
Cassius, *Geoffrey Keen*
Casca, *Mark Dignam*
Cicero, *Donald Eccles*
Cinna, *James Wellman*
Decius Brutus, *Robin Lloyd*
Metellus Cimber, *Donald Layne-Smith*
Trebonius, *Ron Haddrick*
Lucius [servant to Brutus], *Barry Warren*
Portia [wife to Brutus], *Joan Miller*
Caius Ligarius, *Toby Robertson*
Artemidorus, *Clive Revill*
Publius and Popilius Lena [Senators],
   William Elmhirst and Simon Carter
Servant to Julius Cæsar, *Thane Bettany*
Servant to Octavius Cæsar, *Robert Arnold*
Servant to Antony, *Derek Mayhew*
Cinna the Poet, *John Murray Scott*
Octavius Cæsar, *Clive Revill*
M. Aemil. Lepidus, *James Wellman*
Lucilius, *Ron Haddrick*
Titinius, *Donald Eccles*
Messala, *Robin Lloyd*
Varro, *Julian Glover*
Claudius, *John Grayson*
Young Cato, *Robert Arnold*
Clitus, *Thane Bettany*
Dardanius, *Derek Mayhew*
Volumnius, *Donald Layne-Smith*
Strato, *Peter Palmer*
Pindarus [slave to Cassius], *Rex Robinson*
Another Poet, *Toby Robertson*
An Officer to Octavius Cæsar, *Edward Caddick*
Soldiers in Antony's army, *Peter Cellier,*
   Henry Davies and John Davidson

Citizens, Attendants and Soldiers: *Molly Tapper,*
Stephanie Bidmead, Mavis Edwards, Elizabeth Evans,
Pamela Taylor, John Murray Scott, Kenneth Gilbert,
John Salway, Gordon Souter, Roy Spencer,
Gordon Wright, Howard Baker, Christopher Bond,
Michael Saunders, Peter Whitmarsh

18. *Richard Johnson as Mark Antony*

Directed by GLEN BYAM SHAW
Scenery and Costumes by MOTLEY
Music by ANTONY HOPKINS
Fights arranged by BERNARD HEPTON
Lighting by PETER STREULI

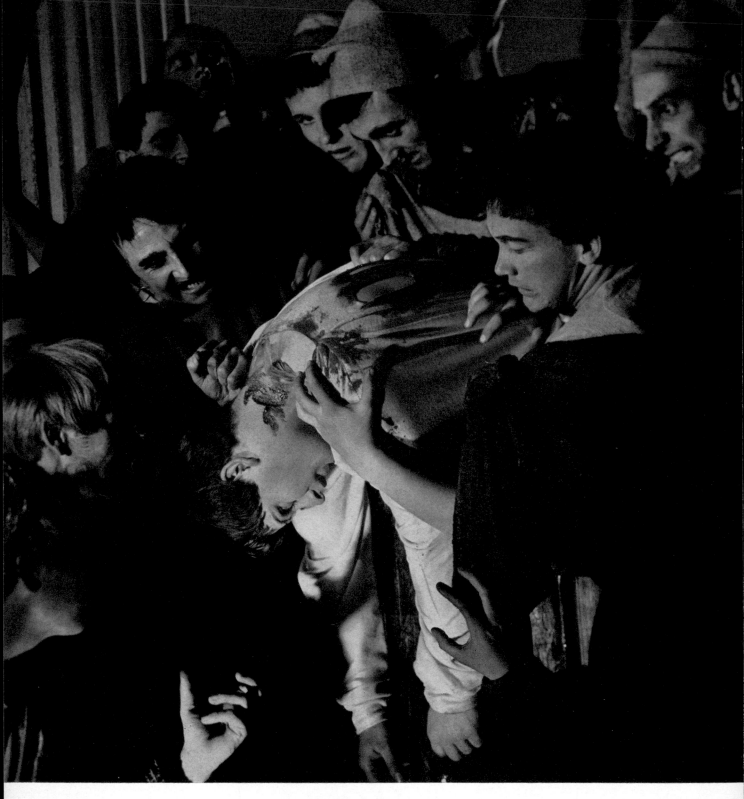

19. Citizens [Act III, Scene 3]
Tear him, tear him!

20. Brutus [Act IV, Scene
Judge me, you gods! wrong I mine enemies?
And, if not so, how should I wrong a brothe

1957

CYMBELINE

A Gentleman, *Thane Bettany*
Lords of Cymbeline's Court, *Peter Cellier
and Barry Warren*
The Queen [wife to Cymbeline], *Joan Miller*
Posthumus Leonatus [husband to Imogen],
Richard Johnson
Imogen [daughter to Cymbeline by a former
Queen], *Peggy Ashcroft*
Cymbeline [King of Britain], *Robert Harris*
Pisanio [servant to Posthumus], *Mark Dignam*
Cloten [son to the Queen by a former husband],
Clive Revill
Helen [a lady attending on Imogen], *Molly Tapper*
Iachimo [an Italian], *Geoffrey Keen*
Philario [an Italian, friend to Posthumus],
Donald Layne-Smith
A Frenchman, *Brian Bedford*
Cornelius [a physician], *James Wellman*
A Singer, *Rex Robinson*
A Councillor attending on Cymbeline,
William Elmhirst
Caius Lucius [General of the Roman forces],
Donald Eccles
Belarius [a banished lord, known as Morgan],
Cyril Luckham
Guiderius and Arviragus [sons to Cymbeline, but
supposed sons to Morgan, known as Polydore
and Cadwal], *Robert Arnold and Brian Bedford*
A Roman Captain, *Derek Mayhew*
British Officers, *Peter Palmer, Donald Layne-Smith
and Simon Carter*
Sicilius Leonatus [father to Posthumus – apparition],
Toby Robertson
His Wife [mother to Posthumus – apparition],
Molly Tapper
British Soldiers, *Julian Glover and John Grayson*
A Gaoler, *Julian Glover*

Lords, Ladies, Servants, Guards; a Spaniard, a
Dutchman; Officers and Soldiers, British and Roman;
Apparitions: *Mavis Edwards, Elizabeth Evans,
Pamela Taylor, Eileen Atkins, Antony Brown,
John Murray Scott, Edward Caddick, John Davidson,
Henry Davies, Kenneth Gilbert, Norman Miller,
John Salway, Gordon Souter, Roy Spencer,
Gordon Wright, Christopher Bond, Michael Saunders,
Peter Whitmarsh*

Directed by PETER HALL
Scenery and costumes by LILA DE NOBILI
Music by RAYMOND LEPPARD
Lighting by MICHAEL NORTHEN

22. Geoffrey Keen as Iachimo

23. Richard Johnson as Posthumus Leonatus

*1. Peggy Ashcroft as Imogen,
live Revill as Cloten*

24. Guiderius [Act IV, Scene 2]

. . . Why, he but sleeps.
If he be gone he'll make his grave a bed;
With female fairies will his tomb be haunted
And worms will not come to thee

Cymbeline [Act III, Scene 1]

w say, what would Augustus Cæsar with us?

27. *Iachimo [Act II, Scene 2]*
. . . Cytherea,
How bravely thou becom'st thy bed!

1957, and Theatre Royal, Drury Lane, London

THE TEMPEST

From December 5th, 1957, this production played a seven-week London season at the Theatre Royal, Drury Lane, presented with Tennent Productions.

The Master of a Ship, *Peter Palmer*
A Boatswain, *Ron Haddrick*
Alonso [King of Naples], *Robert Harris*
Antonio [usurping Duke of Milan, brother to Prospero], *Mark Dignam*
Gonzalo [an honest old counsellor], *Cyril Luckham*
Sebastian [brother to Alonso], *Robin Lloyd*
Adrian [a lord], *Toby Robertson*
Miranda [daughter to Prospero], *Doreen Aris*
Prospero [the right Duke of Milan], *John Gielgud*
Ariel [an airy spirit], *Brian Bedford*
Caliban [a savage and deformed slave], *Alec Clunes*
Ferdinand [son to the King of Naples], *Richard Johnson*
Trinculo [a jester], *Clive Revill*
Stephano [a drunken butler], *Patrick Wymark*
Iris, Ceres and Juno [presented by spirits], *Jane Wenham, Stephanie Bidmead and Joan Miller*

Mariners, Nymphs, Reapers, and others presented by Spirits: *Mavis Edwards, Elizabeth Evans, Pamela Taylor, Eileen Atkins, Rex Robinson, Robert Arnold, Thane Bettany, Antony Brown, Derek Mayhew, John Murray Scott, Barry Warren, Edward Caddick, Simon Carter, John Davidson, Henry Davies, William Elmhirst, Kenneth Gilbert, Julian Glover, John Grayson, Norman Miller, John Salway, Gordon Souter, Roy Spencer, Gordon Wright*

During the London season *Olive Gregg* played Iris and *Ellen McIntosh*, Juno

Directed by PETER BROOK
Designs and music by PETER BROOK, with Michael Northen, Kegan Smith and William Blezard
Choreography by RAIMONDA ORSELLI

28. Brian Bedford as Ariel   *29. John Gielgud as Prospero*

30. *Alec Clunes as Caliban, Patrick Wymark as Stephano, Clive Revill as Trinculo*

31. Richard Johnson as Ferdinand, Doreen Aris as Miranda

32. Gonzalo [Act II, Scene 2]
. . . Now, good angels
Preserve the King!

33. Juno [Act IV, Scene 1]

                   . . . Go with me
To bless this twain, that they may prosperous be,
And honour'd in their issue

34. Caliban [Act I, Scene 2]
This island's mine, by Sycorax my mother,
Which thou tak'st from me

35. Laurence Olivier as Titus Andronicus, Vivien Leigh as Lavinia

The Continent and London, 1957

TITUS ANDRONICUS

This production, which was first presented during the 1955 Stratford season, played a three-month Continental tour in 1957, finishing in London (Stoll Theatre, 1st July – 3rd August). It visited Paris (15th-25th May), Venice (28th-30th May), Belgrade (2nd-4th June), Zagreb (7th-8th June), Vienna (12th-15th June), Warsaw (18th-21st June).

Saturninus [son to the late Emperor of Rome], *Frank Thring*
Bassianus [his brother], *Ralph Michael*
Marcus Andronicus [tribune of the people and brother to Titus], *Alan Webb*
A Roman Captain, *Michael Blakemore*
Titus Andronicus, *Laurence Olivier*
Lucius, Quintus, Martius and Mutius [his sons], *Basil Hoskins, Leon Eagles, John McGregor and Ian Holm*
Tamora [Queen of the Goths], *Maxine Audley*
Alarbus, Chiron and Demetrius [her sons], *Michael Murray, Kevin Miles and Lee Montague*
Aaron [a Moor], *Anthony Quayle*
Lavinia [daughter to Titus Andronicus], *Vivien Leigh*
Aemilius [a noble Roman], *William Devlin*
A Messenger, *Bernard Kay*
Young Lucius [son to Lucius], *Meurig Wyn-Jones*
A Nurse, *Rosalind Atkinson*
A Clown, *Edward Atienza*
First Goth, *Paul Hardwick*
Second Goth, *David Conville*
Third Goth, *Patrick Stephens*
Publius [son to Marcus Andronicus], *Neville Jason*
Caius, *Gordon Gardner*
A Roman, *Hugh Cross*

Kinsmen of Titus, Priests, Judges, Soldiers, Huntsmen, Citizens and Goths : *Frances Leak, Ellen McIntosh, Moira Redmond, Victoria Watts, James Greene, Terence Greenidge, Alan Haywood, Ewan Hooper, Peter James, George Little, Grant Reddick, John Standing, Peter Whitbread, Ian White*

Directed by PETER BROOK
Designs and music by PETER BROOK, with Michael Northen, Desmond Heeley and William Blezard

36. *Anthony Quayle as Aaron, Maxine Audley as Tamora*

37. Titus [Act III, Scene 1]
Let's kiss and part, for we have much to do

38. Vivien Leigh as Lavinia

1958
ROMEO AND JULIET

Chorus, *Anthony Nicholls*

Sampson, Gregory, Peter, Potpan, Anthony and Old Man [servants to Capulet], *Peter Palmer, Julian Glover, Ian Holm, John Grayson, Edward de Souza and Eric Holmes*

Abraham and Balthasar [servants to Montague], *Thane Bettany and Kenneth Gilbert*

Benvolio [nephew to Montague] *Paul Hardwick*

Tybalt [nephew to Lady Capulet], *Ron Haddrick*

Tybalt's Page, *Gordon Souter*

Capulet, *Mark Dignam*

Lady Capulet, *Rachel Kempson*

Cousin Capulet, *Donald Eccles*

Montague, *Donald Layne-Smith*

Lady Montague, *Stephanie Bidmead*

Prince of Verona, *Anthony Nicholls*

Romeo, *Richard Johnson*

Paris [kinsman to the Prince], *Michael Meacham*

Paris's Page, *Roy Spencer*

Juliet, *Dorothy Tutin*

Nurse to Juliet, *Angela Baddeley*

Mercutio, *Edward Woodward*

Mercutio's Page, *John Davidson*

Friar Laurence, *Cyril Luckham*

Friar John, *Edward de Souza*

An Apothecary, *Donald Eccles*

First Watch, *Antony Brown*

Second Watch, *John Salway*

Prince's Guards, *Roy Dotrice, Roger Bizley and Paxton Whitehead*

Citizens of Verona and Mantua, Guests, Musicians, Servants and Watchmen: *Miranda Connell, Mavis Edwards, Eileen Atkins, Pamela Taylor, Zoe Caldwell, William Elmhirst, Peter Anderson, Stephen Thorne*

Directed by GLEN BYAM SHAW
Scenery and costumes by MOTLEY
Music by LESLIE BRIDGEWATER
Fights arranged by BERNARD HEPTON
Dances arranged by PAULINE GRANT
Lighting by PATRICK DONNELL

40. *Cyril Luckham as Friar Laurence*

41. *Edward Woodward as Mercutio*

42. *Mark Dignam as Capulet*

29. *Angela Baddeley as the Nurse, Dorothy Tutin as Juliet, Richard Johnson as Romeo*

43. *Ron Haddrick as Tybalt*

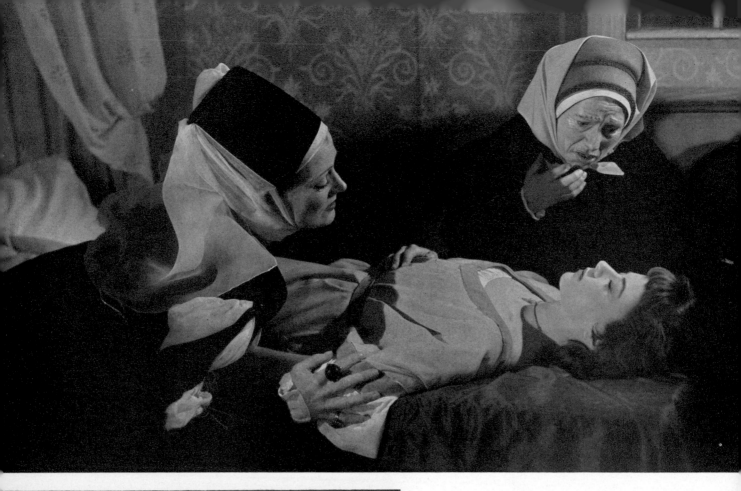

44. *Lady Capulet [Act IV, Scene 5]*
O me, O me! My child, my only life,
Revive, look up, or I will die with thee!

45. *Anthony Nicholls as the Prince of Verona*

46. *Ian Holm as Peter*

47. *Romeo [Act I, Scene 5]*
What lady's that which doth enrich the hand
Of yonder knight?

48. Dorothy Tutin as Juliet

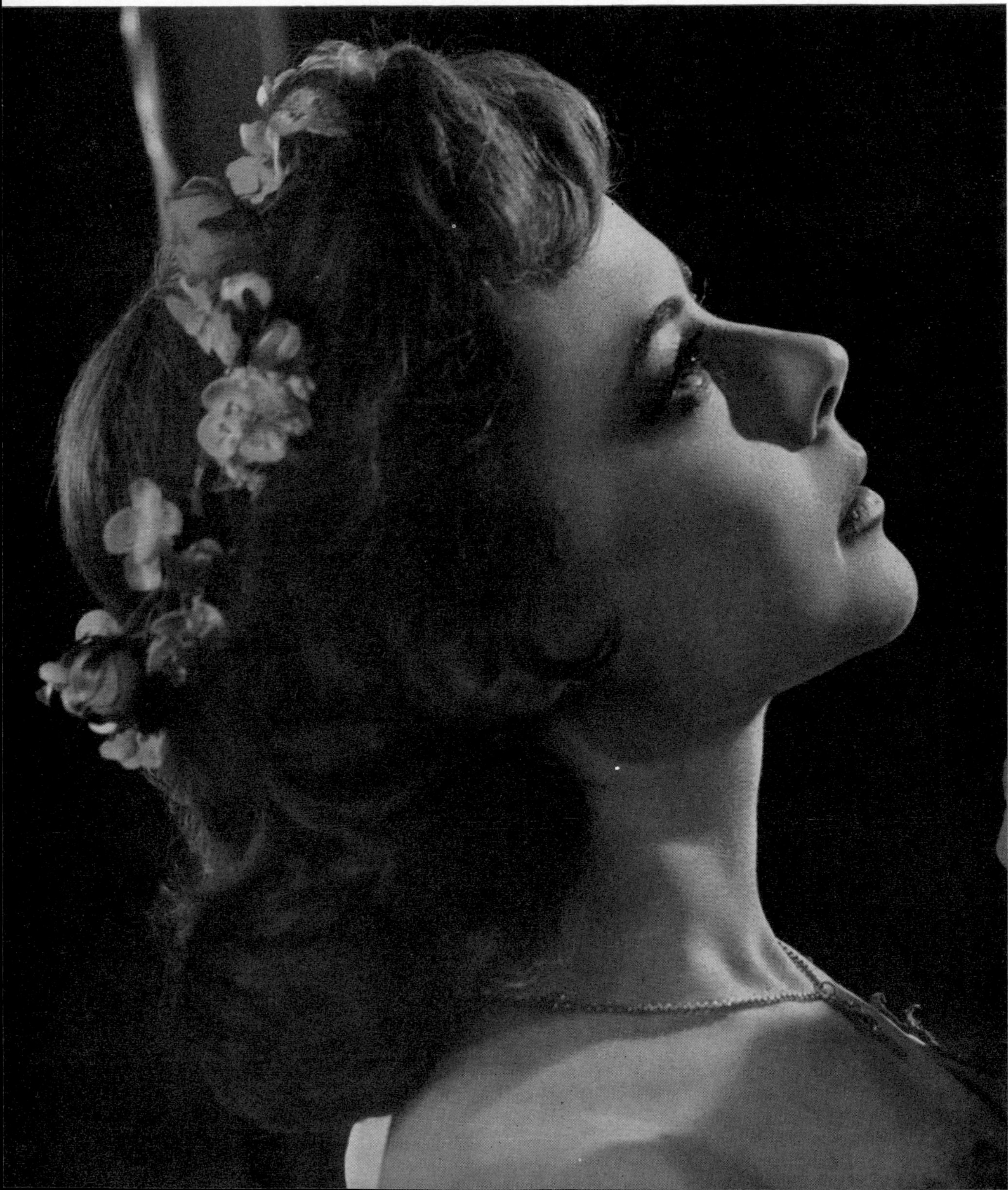

49. *Richard Johnson as Romeo*

1958

TWELFTH NIGHT

Orsino [Duke of Illyria], *Michael Meacham*
Curio and Valentine [gentlemen attending on
   the Duke], *Roy Spencer and Kenneth Gilbert*
Viola, *Dorothy Tutin*
A Sea Captain, *Antony Brown*
Sir Toby Belch [Olivia's kinsman], *Patrick Wymark*
Maria [Olivia's gentlewoman], *Miranda Connell*
Sir Andrew Aguecheek, *Richard Johnson*
Feste [Olivia's clown], *Cyril Luckham*
Olivia, *Geraldine McEwan*
Malvolio [Olivia's steward], *Mark Dignam*
Fabian [servant to Olivia], *Peter Palmer*
Antonio [a sea captain], *Ron Haddrick*
Sebastian, *Ian Holm*
Servant to Olivia, *Gordon Souter*
Officers, *Paul Hardwick, Roy Dotrice
   and John Grayson*
Priest, *Donald Layne-Smith*

Ladies, Lords, Servants and Sailors: *Mavis Edwards,
Zoe Caldwell, John Davidson, William Elmhirst,
Julian Glover, John Salway, Peter Anderson,
Roger Bizley, Edward de Souza, Eric Holmes,
Stephen Thorne, Paxton Whitehead*

Directed by PETER HALL
Scenery and Costumes by LILA DE NOBILI
Music by RAYMOND LEPPARD
Dance arranged by PAULINE GRANT
Lighting by MICHAEL NORTHEN

*. Dorothy Tutin as Viola,
ark Dignam as Malvolio*

51. Geraldine McEwan as Olivia

52. Richard Johnson as Aguecheek,
Cyril Luckham as Feste,
Patrick Wymark as Sir Toby Belch

54. *Captain* [*Act I, Scene 2*]
Be you his eunuch and your mute I'll be

55. *Michael Meacham as Orsino*

56. Miranda Connell as Maria

57. Antonio [Act III, Scene 4]
Put up your sword. If this young gentleman
Have done offence, I take the fault on me

58. *Googie Withers as Gertrude, Michael Redgrave as Hamlet*

1958

HAMLET

Francisco, *Paxton Whitehead*
Barnardo, *Julian Glover*
Marcellus, *Antony Brown*
Horatio, *Ron Haddrick*
Ghost of Hamlet's father, *Anthony Nicholls*
Hamlet, *Michael Redgrave*
Polonius, *Cyril Luckham*
Claudius [King of Denmark], *Mark Dignam*
Gertrude [Queen of Denmark], *Googie Withers*
Cornelius and Voltimand [Ambassadors],
   John Salway and Eric Holmes
Osric, *Thane Bettany*
Laertes [son of Polonius], *Edward Woodward*
Ophelia [daughter of Polonius], *Dorothy Tutin*
Reynaldo, *Ian Holm*
Rosencrantz, *Paul Hardwick*
Guildenstern, *Michael Meacham*
First Player, *Patrick Wymark*
Player King, *Donald Layne-Smith*
Player Queen, *Stephanie Bidmead*
Second Player, *Ian Holm*
Fortinbras, *John Grayson*
A Captain, *Peter Palmer*
Lady [attending the Queen], *Eileen Atkins*
Courtier, *William Elmhirst*
Royal Servant, *Roy Spencer*
Sailor, *Gordon Souter*
Gravedigger, *Donald Eccles*
Sacristan, *Julian Glover*
Priest, *Kenneth Gilbert*

Courtiers, Ladies, Servants, Players, Soldiers
and Rebels: *Miranda Connell, Mavis Edwards,*
Pamela Taylor, Zoe Caldwell, John Davidson,
Peter Anderson, Roger Bizley, Edward de Souza,
Roy Dotrice, Stephen Thorne

Directed by GLEN BYAM SHAW
Scenery and costumes by MOTLEY
Music by ANTONY HOPKINS
Fight arranged by BERNARD HEPTON
   and JOHN GREENWOOD
Mime arranged by NORMAN AYRTON
Lighting by PATRICK DONNELL

59. Dorothy Tutin as Ophelia

61. *Edward Woodward as Laertes*

62. *Ron Haddrick as Horatio*

OPPOSITE: 60. *Michael Redgrave as Hamlet, Anthony Nicholls as the Ghost*

63. *Paul Hardwick and Michael Meacham as Rosencrantz and Guildenstern*

64. *Donald Eccles as the Gravedigger*

65. *Dorothy Tutin as Ophelia, Cyril Luckham as Polonius*

Michael Redgrave
as Hamlet

PERICLES

Gower, *Edric Connor*
Antiochus [King of Antioch], *Paul Hardwick*
Daughter of Antiochus, *Zoe Caldwell*
Thaliard [a Lord of Antioch], *Edward Woodward*
Antioch Messenger, *Roger Bizley*
Pericles [Prince of Tyre], *Richard Johnson*
Helicanus [a Lord of Tyre], *Cyril Luckham*
Lords of Tyre, *Thane Bettany and Kenneth Gilbert*
Cleon [Governor of Tarsus], *Donald Eccles*
Dionyza [wife to Cleon], *Rachel Kempson*
Tarsus Messenger, *John Grayson*
First Fisherman, *Julian Glover*
Second Fisherman, *Eric Holmes*
Third Fisherman, *John Davidson*
Simonides [King of Pentapolis], *Mark Dignam*
Thaisa [daughter of Simonides], *Stephanie Bidmead*
Lychorida [Nurse], *Mavis Edwards*
Marshall of Pentapolis, *Donald Layne-Smith*
Pentapolis Lords, *John Salway, William Elmhirst
    and Roy Spencer*
Cerimon [a Lord of Ephesus], *Anthony Nicholls*
Philemon [servant of Cerimon], *Kenneth Gilbert*
Ephesus Gentlemen, *Roy Dotrice and Roy Spencer*
Ephesus Servant, *Peter Anderson*
Marina [daughter of Thaisa], *Geraldine McEwan*
Leonine [servant to Dionyza], *Peter Palmer*
Pirates, *Gordon Souter, Edward de Souza
    and Stephen Thorne*
Bawd, *Angela Baddeley*
Boult, *Patrick Wymark*
Pandar, *Donald Layne-Smith*
Mytilene Gentlemen, *William Elmhirst
    and Edward de Souza*
Lysimachus [Governor of Mytilene],
    Michael Meacham
Diana, *Eileen Atkins*

Sailors, Knights, Citizens and Priestesses:
*Miranda Connell, Eileen Atkins, Elizabeth Evans,
Zoe Caldwell, Thane Bettany, John Davidson,
William Elmhirst, Kenneth Gilbert, Julian Glover,
John Grayson, John Salway, Gordon Souter,
Roy Spencer, Peter Anderson, Roger Bizley,
Edward de Souza, Roy Dotrice, Eric Holmes,
Stephen Thorne, Paxton Whitehead*

67. Richard Johnson as Pericles

68. Patrick Wymark as Boult, Geraldine McEwan as Marina

Directed by TONY RICHARDSON
Scenery and costumes by LOUDON SAINTHILL
Music and Sound by ROBERTO GERHARD
Dance arranged by PAULINE GRANT
Lighting by MICHAEL NORTHEN

74. *Angela Baddeley as the Bawd*

OPPOSITE PAGE: 69. *Edric Connor as Gower*

70. *Paul Hardwick as Antiochus*
71. *Mark Dignam as Simonides*
72. *Rachel Kempson as Dionyza*
73. *Michael Meacham as Lysimachus*

OPPOSITE:

75. *Pericles [Act I, Scene 4]*
　　　. . . Arise, I pray you, rise.
We do not look for reverence, but for love

76. *Cerimon [Act V, Scene 3]*
Noble sir,
If you have told Diana's altar true,
This is your wife

77. *Pericles [Act I, Scene 1]*
　　　. . . But, O you powers
That give heaven countless eyes to view men's acts,
Why cloud they not their sights perpetually,
If this be true, which makes me pale to read it?

79. *Rachel Kempson as Ursula, Geraldine McEwan as Hero, Zoe Caldwell as Margaret*

1958

MUCH ADO
ABOUT NOTHING

Leonato [Governor of Messina], *Cyril Luckham*
Beatrice [his niece], *Googie Withers*
Hero [his daughter], *Geraldine McEwan*
Messenger, *Thane Bettany*
Don Pedro [Prince of Arragon], *Anthony Nicholls*
Don John [his brother], *Richard Johnson*
Benedick, *Michael Redgrave*
Claudio, *Edward Woodward*
Antonio [brother of Leonato], *Donald Layne-Smith*
Conrade, *Julian Glover*
Borachio, *Peter Palmer*
Ursula, *Rachel Kempson*
Margaret, *Zoe Caldwell*
Balthasar, *Edward de Souza*
Dogberry, *Patrick Wymark*

Verges, *Ian Holm*
First Watch, *Antony Brown*
Second Watch, *John Davidson*
Third Watch, *John Salway*
Fourth Watch, *Eric Holmes*
Friar Francis, *Donald Eccles*
Sexton, *William Elmhirst*
Benedick's Servant, *Roy Spencer*
Leonato's Servant, *Gordon Souter*
A Barber, *Roger Bizley*

Soldiers, Servants, Citizens and Guests:
Stephanie Bidmead, Mavis Edwards, Eileen Atkins,
Pamela Taylor, John Grayson, Roy Dotrice,
Stephen Thorne, Paxton Whitehead, Richard Rudd

Directed by DOUGLAS SEALE
Scenery by TANYA MOISEIWITSCH
Costumes by MOTLEY
Music by CHRISTOPHER WHELEN
Dances arranged by PAULINE GRANT
Lighting by MAURICE DANIELS

78. *Googie Withers as Beatrice,*
Michael Redgrave as Benedick

81. *Leonato* [*Act IV, Scene 1*]
        . . . Friar, it cannot be.
Thou seest that all the grace that she hath left
Is that she will not add to her damnation
A sin of perjury

82. Googie Withers
as Beatrice

83. Patrick Wyma
as Dogber

85. Donald Layne-Sm
as Anto

84. Ian Holm
as Verges

86. Anthony Nicholls
as Don Pedro

OPPOSITE PA
87. Benedick [Act I, Sc.
If Signior Leonato
be her father,
she would not have
his head
on her shoulders for
all Messina,
as like him as she is

RUSSIA 1957-58

At the end of the 1958 Stratford season the company made a triumphant visit to Russia, playing two weeks in Leningrad – the first English company to act there since the Revolution – and two weeks in Moscow. They presented *Romeo and Juliet*, *Twelfth Night* and *Hamlet* in each city.

90. *Standing on the frozen river Neva in Leningrad: Geraldine McEwan, Dorothy Tutin, Miranda Connell and Zoe Caldwell*

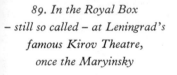

89. *In the Royal Box – still so called – at Leningrad's famous Kirov Theatre, once the Maryinsky*

POSITE PAGE: 88. *Leningrad: Rachel Kempson, ichael Redgrave and gela Baddeley with Coral owne (who joined the company play Gertrude throughout s visit to Russia)*

91. *Michael Redgrave, Richard Johnson, Dorothy Tutin and Geraldine McEwan meet the two prima ballerinas at the Kirov Theatre*

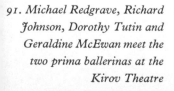

92. *After the first night at the Moscow Art Theatre:*
Richard Johnson (Romeo) and Dorothy Tutin (Juliet)

93. *Twelfth Night at the Moscow Art Theatre:*
the company acknowledges a rapturous reception

94. *The packed firstnight audience in Leningrad.*
Stephen Arlen (of the British Council, sponsors
of the visit), Lady Flower, Michael Redgrave,
Coral Browne and Peter Hall are seen in the
front row

95. *Posters at the Moscow Art Theatre
advertise the visit*

96. *Backstage in Leningrad:
Glen Byam Shaw with Richard Johnson,
Dorothy Tutin, Peter Hall and Russian theatre officials*

97. *In the corridor of the night express from Leningrad
to Moscow: Dorothy Tutin, Stephen Arlen,
Anthony Nicholls*

98. *Leaving London Airport: the press take pictures
as Dorothy Tutin boards the charter plane which
flew the entire company non-stop to Moscow*

1959
OTHELLO

Roderigo, *Peter Woodthorpe*
Iago, *Sam Wanamaker*
Brabantio, *Paul Hardwick*
Othello, *Paul Robeson*
Cassio, *Albert Finney*
Duke of Venice, *Ian Holm*
Lodovico, *Edward de Souza*
Gratiano, *Donald Layne-Smith*
Desdemona, *Mary Ure*
Emilia, *Angela Baddeley*
Montano, *Julian Glover*
First Montano Officer, *David Buck*
Second Montano Officer, *Roy Dotrice*
Third Montano Officer, *Kenneth Gilbert*
Herald, *Stephen Thorne*
Bianca, *Zoe Caldwell*

Venetian Citizens, Senators, Officers, Messengers,
Soldiers, Citizens of Cyprus: *Georgine Anderson,*
Roger Bizley, Charles Borromel, Michael Graham Cox,
Christopher Cruise, Jon Dennis, Mavis Edwards,
Nicholas Hawtrey, Norman Henry, Edna Landor,
Peter Mason, Dan Meaden, Vanessa Redgrave,
Diana Rigg, Richard Rudd, Robert Russell, Don Smith,
Roy Spencer, Malcolm Taylor, Dave Thomas,
Stephen Thorne

Directed by TONY RICHARDSON
Scenery and costumes by LOUDON SAINTHILL
Lighting by MICHAEL NORTHEN

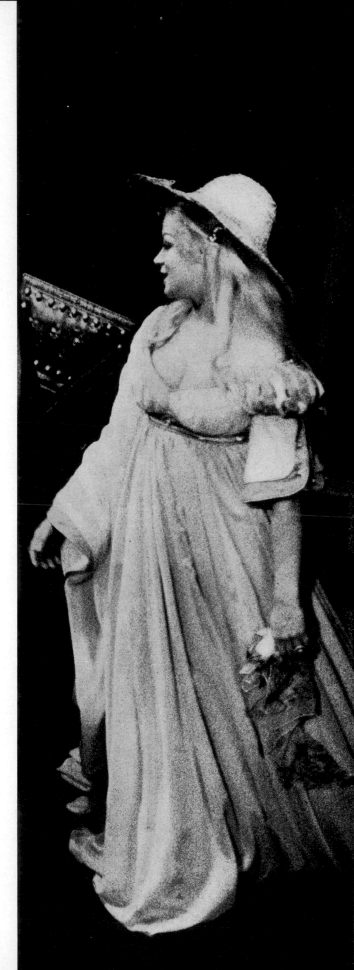

. *Paul Robeson as Othello,*
ım Wanamaker as Iago

100. Mary Ure
as Desdemona

101. *Paul Hardwick as Brabantio*
103. *Kenneth Gilbert as a Montano Officer, Julian Glover as Montano*

102. *Ian Holm as the Duke of Venice*
104. *Albert Finney as Cassio*

105. *Angela Baddeley as Emilia*

OVERLEAF:
107. *Desdemona* [*Act IV, Scene 2*]
Alas the heavy day! Why do you weep?

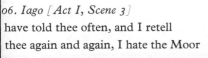
106. *Iago* [*Act I, Scene 3*]
have told thee often, and I retell
thee again and again, I hate the Moor

109. *The Duke of Florence reviews his troops*

1959

ALL'S WELL
THAT ENDS WELL

Countess of Rossillion, *Edith Evans*
Bertram [her son], *Edward de Souza*
Helena [her ward], *Zoe Caldwell*
Lafeu, *Anthony Nicholls*
Rinaldo [steward to the Countess], *Donald Eccles*
Parolles, *Cyril Luckham*
Groom, *Malcolm Taylor*
King of France, *Robert Hardy*
Longaville, *Paul Hardwick*
Dumain, *Michael Blakemore*
First Officer, *Kenneth Gilbert*
Second Officer, *Roy Spencer*
Major Domo, *Michael Graham Cox*
Footmen, *Roger Bizley, Richard Rudd*
    and Dave Thomas

Duke of Florence, *Donald Layne-Smith*
Widow, *Angela Baddeley*
Diana [her daughter], *Priscilla Morgan*
Mariana [her neighbour], *Mavis Edwards*
First Soldier, *Peter Woodthorpe*
Gentleman, *Stephen Thorne*

Ladies, Officers, Diplomats, Soldiers and Neighbours:
Georgine Anderson, Charles Borromel, David Buck,
Christopher Cruise, Jon Dennis, Nicholas Hawtrey,
Norman Henry, Edna Landor, Peter Mason,
Dan Meaden, Vanessa Redgrave, Diana Rigg,
Robert Russell, Don Smith

Directed by TYRONE GUTHRIE
Scenery and Costumes by TANYA MOISEIWITSCH
Music by JOHN GARDNER
Dances arranged by PAULINE GRANT
Lighting by MAURICE DANIELS

108. Zoe Caldwell as Helena,
Edith Evans as the Countess of Rossillion

III. Lafeu [Act II, Scene 3]
Why, he's able to lead her a coranto

II2. Second Lord [Act II, Scene 1]
Health, at your bidding, serve your
Majesty!

OPPOSITE:
IIo. Helena [Act III, Scene 5]
Which is the Frenchman?

114. First Soldier [Act IV, Scene 3]
When he swears oaths, bid him drop gold, and tak

113. Robert Hardy as the King of France

115. Angela Baddeley as the Widow

116. Parolles [Act IV, Scene 1]
I would the cutting of my garments would
serve the turn

117. Countess [Act I, Scene 1]
. . . Love all, trust a few,
Do wrong to none . . .

1959
A MIDSUMMER NIGHT'S DREAM

Theseus [Duke of Athens], *Anthony Nicholls*
Hippolyta [Queen of the Amazons], *Stephanie Bidmead*
Philostrate [Master of the Revels],
    Donald Layne-Smith
Egeus [father to Hermia], *Roy Dotrice*
Hermia, *Priscilla Morgan*
Lysander, *Albert Finney*
Demetrius, *Edward de Souza*
Helena, *Vanessa Redgrave*
Quince [a carpenter], *Cyril Luckham*
Bottom [a weaver], *Charles Laughton*
Flute [a bellows mender], *Peter Woodthorpe*
Starveling [a tailor], *Donald Eccles*
Snout [a tinker], *Michael Blakemore*
Snug [a joiner], *Julian Glover*
Puck [or Robin Goodfellow], *Ian Holm*
A Fairy, *Zoe Caldwell*
Oberon [King of the Fairies], *Robert Hardy*
Titania [Queen of the Fairies], *Mary Ure*
Fairies, *Mavis Edwards, Georgine Anderson,*
    Judith Downes, Margaret O'Keefe, Jean Owen,
    Malcolm Ranson and Michael Scoble

Attendants on Theseus, Hippolyta and Oberon:
Roger Bizley, Charles Borromel, David Buck,
Michael Graham Cox, Christopher Cruise,
Jon Dennis, Nicholas Hawtrey, Norman Henry,
Edna Landor, Peter Mason, Dan Meaden, Diana Rigg,
Richard Rudd, Robert Russell, Don Smith,
Dave Thomas, Stephen Thorne

Directed by PETER HALL
Scenery and Costumes by LILA DE NOBILI
Music by RAYMOND LEPPARD
Dances arranged by PAULINE GRANT
Lighting by MICHAEL NORTHEN

119. *Zoe Caldwell as a Fairy, Ian Holm as Puck*

8. *Charles Laughton as Bottom*

120. Robert Hardy as Oberon, Mary Ure as Titania

121. Hermia [Act III, Scene

Why will you suffer her to flout me thus

Let me come to her

122. Egeus [Act IV, Scene 1]
I beg the law, the law upon his head

123. Cyril Luckham as Quince

4. Quince [Act V, Scene 1]

his man, with lanthorn, dog, and bush of thorn,
esenteth Moonshine

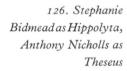

126. Stephanie
Bidmead as Hippolyta,
Anthony Nicholls as
Theseus

125. Donald Layne-
Smith as Philostrate

1959
CORIOLANUS

Caius Marcius Coriolanus, *Laurence Olivier*
Menenius, *Harry Andrews*
Titus Lartius and Cominius [Roman Generals],
    Donald Eccles and Paul Hardwick
Junius Brutus and Sicinius Velutus [Tribunes],
    Peter Woodthorpe and Robert Hardy
Roman Senator, *Michael Blakemore*
First Roman Citizen, *Albert Finney*
Second Roman Citizen, *Julian Glover*
Third Roman Citizen, *Roy Dotrice*
Fourth Roman Citizen, *Ian Holm*
Fifth Roman Citizen, *Michael Graham Cox*
Sixth Roman Citizen, *Stephen Thorne*
Seventh Roman Citizen, *Dan Meaden*
Senate Officers, *Donald Layne-Smith
    and Edward de Souza*
First Aedile, *Kenneth Gilbert*
Second Aedile, *Peter Mason*
Roman Citizens, *Stephanie Bidmead,
    Georgine Anderson, Edna Landnor,
    Diana Rigg and Michael Scoble*
Roman Soldiers, *Roy Spencer, Richard Rudd,
    Christopher Cruise, Jon Dennis, Don Smith
    and Malcolm Taylor*
Volumnia, *Edith Evans*
Virgilia, *Mary Ure*
Valeria, *Vanessa Redgrave*
Gentlewoman, *Mavis Edwards*
Young Marcius, *Malcolm Ranson*
Tullus Aufidius [Volscian General], *Anthony Nicholls*
Lieutenant to Aufidius, *Edward de Souza*
First Volscian Senator, *Donald Layne-Smith*
Second Volscian Senator, *Charles Borromel*
Third Volscian Senator, *Norman Henry*
Volscian Citizen, *Nicholas Hawtrey*
First Aufidius Servant, *Michael Graham Cox*
Second Aufidius Servant, *Roy Dotrice*
Third Aufidius Servant, *Ian Holm*
First Volscian Sentinel, *Dave Thomas*
Second Volscian Sentinel, *Robert Russell*
First Volscian Conspirator, *David Buck*
Second Volscian Conspirator, *Roger Bizley*

Directed by PETER HALL
Setting by BORIS ARONSON
Costumes by RIETTE STURGE MOORE
Music by ROBERTO GERHARD
Fights arranged by BERNARD HEPTON
    and JOHN GREENWOOD
Lighting by MICHAEL NORTHEN

128. Harry Andrews as Menenius

27. Laurence Olivier as Coriolanus

129. *Seventh Citizen [Act II, Scene 3]*
Therefore let him be consul

130. *Cominius [Act I, Scene 9]*
. . . Caius Marcius Coriolanus.
Bear th' addition nobly ever!

131. *First Citizen*
[Act I, Scene 1]
You are all resolv'd rather
to die than to famish?

132. *Edith Evans as Volumnia*

133. *Aufidius [Act IV, Scene 5]*
O Marcius, Marcius!
Each word thou hast spoke hath
    weeded from my heart
A root of ancient envy

134. Volumnia

[Act V, Scene 3]

Down, ladies; let us shame
him with our knees

1959
KING LEAR

Earl of Kent, *Anthony Nicholls*
Earl of Gloucester, *Cyril Luckham*
Edmund, *Robert Hardy*
King Lear, *Charles Laughton*
Goneril, *Stephanie Bidmead*
Regan, *Angela Baddeley*
Cordelia, *Zoe Caldwell*
Duke of Albany, *Julian Glover*
Duke of Cornwall, *Paul Hardwick*
King of France, *Edward de Souza*
Duke of Burgundy, *Roy Dotrice*
Edgar, *Albert Finney*
Knight to Lear, *Michael Blakemore*
Oswald, *Peter Woodthorpe*
Fool, *Ian Holm*
Curan, *Stephen Thorne*
First Regan Servant, *Michael Graham Cox*
Second Regan Servant, *Roger Bizley*
Third Regan Servant, *David Buck*
Gloucester's Tenant, *Donald Eccles*
Doctor, *Kenneth Gilbert*
Herald, *Roy Spencer*
Edmund's Captain, *Peter Mason*
Herald's Trumpeter, *Stanley Wheeler*
Edgar's Trumpeter, *Arthur Allaby*
Cordelia Messenger, *Don Smith*
Regan Soldier, *Richard Rudd*
Edmund Standard Bearer, *Dave Thomas*

Counsellors, Knights, Squires, Servants, Tenants, and Soldiers: *Mavis Edwards, Georgine Anderson, Edna Landor, Diana Rigg, Charles Borromel, Christopher Cruise, Jon Dennis, Nicholas Hawtrey, Norman Henry, Dan Meaden, Robert Russell, Malcolm Taylor, Michael Scoble*

Directed by GLEN BYAM SHAW
Scenery and costumes by MOTLEY
Music by ANTONY HOPKINS
Fights arranged by BERNARD HEPTON
Lighting by MICHAEL NORTHEN

135. Lear [Act III, Scene 2]
Crack nature's moulds, all germens spill at once,
That make ingrateful man!

138. Lear [Act I, Scene 1]
But goes thy heart with this?

139. Lear [Act V, Scene 3]
Pray you, undo this button

140. Cornwall [Act III, Scene 7]
Out vile jelly!

SHAKESPEARE MEMORIAL THEATRE

Glen Byam Shaw, CBE, Director

Patrick Donnell, DSO, Assistant to the Director

STRATFORD 1957

HOUSE

John Jolley, House Manager
John Goodwin } Press and
Vincent Pearmain } Publicity
Edoardo Milano } Catering Manager
Jeremy Gye } and Assistant
Peter Hampson, Box Office Manager

PRODUCTION

Desmond Hall, Production Manager
Kegan Smith, Costume Supervisor
Fred Jenkins, Chief Construction Carpenter
Gerry Watts, Property Master
Reg Sayle, Scenic Artist

STAGE

Peter Streuli, Stage Director
Maurice Daniels, Assistant Stage Director
Hal Rogers, Stage Manager
Alisoun Browne }
Howard Baker } Assistant Stage Managers
Judy Wright }
Eddie Golding, Stage Carpenter
John Bruce, Chief Electrician
Audrey Sellman, Wardrobe Mistress

THE CONTINENT AND LONDON 1957

[TITUS ANDRONICUS]

Patrick Donnell, Company Manager
Floy Bell, Assistant Manager
Keith Green, Stage Manager
Leonard James, Deputy Stage Manager
Sue Goldsworthy }
Stella Maude } Assistant Stage Managers
Colin Clark }
Raymond Burge, Chief Technician
Clem Batsford, Assistant Technician
Lyn Hope, Wardrobe Mistress
Pat Eagles } Assistants to
Lyn Holm } Wardrobe Mistress
Alec MacDonald, Chief Electrician
John Goodwin } Press and
Vincent Pearmain } Publicity

STRATFORD 1958

HOUSE

John Jolley, Manager and Licensee
John Goodwin } Press and
Vincent Pearmain } Publicity
Edoardo Milano } Catering Manager
Jeremy Gye } and Assistant
Peter Hampson, Box Office Manager

PRODUCTION

Desmond Hall, Production Manager
Kegan Smith, Costume Supervisor
Fred Jenkins, Chief Construction Carpenter
Gerry Watts, Property Master
Reg Sayle, Scenic Artist

STAGE

Maurice Daniels, Stage Director
Hal Rogers }
Alisoun Browne } Stage Managers
Judy Wright }
Leonard James }
Neville Pearson } Assistant Stage Managers
Brian Croft }
Eddie Golding, Stage Carpenter
John Bradley, Chief Electrician
Audrey Sellman, Wardrobe Mistress

THEATRE ROYAL, DRURY LANE, LONDON, 1957

[THE TEMPEST]

Hal Rogers, Stage Manager
Alisoun Browne }
Howard Baker } Assistant Stage Managers
Judy Wright }
John Goodwin } Press and
Vincent Pearmain } Publicity

STRATFORD 1959

HOUSE

John Jolley, Manager and Licensee
Leonard James, House Manager
John Goodwin } Press and
Vincent Pearmain } Publicity
Edoardo Milano } Catering Manager
Maurice Bird } and Assistant
Peter Hampson, Box Office Manager

PRODUCTION

Desmond Hall, Production Manager
Kegan Smith, Costume Supervisor
Fred Jenkins, Chief Construction Carpenter
Gerry Watts, Property Master
Reg Sayle, Scenic Artist

STAGE

Maurice Daniels, Stage Director
Hal Rogers, Deputy Stage Director
Alisoun Browne, Stage Manager
Neville Pearson }
Ann Fosbrooke } Assistant Stage Managers
Brian Croft }
Eddie Golding, Stage Carpenter
John Bradley, Chief Electrician
Audrey Sellman, Wardrobe Mistress

LENINGRAD AND MOSCOW 1958-59

[ROMEO AND JULIET, TWELFTH NIGHT, HAMLET]

Patrick Donnell, Company Manager
Maurice Daniels, Stage Director
Hal Rogers }
Alisoun Browne } Stage Managers
Judy Wright }
Neville Pearson } Assistant Stage Managers
Brian Croft }
Leonard James, Administrator
Floy Bell, Secretary
Douglas Cornelissen, Chief Electrician
Nigel Birch, Assistant Electrician
Clem Batsford }
George Betts } Technicians
Richard O'Halleran }
Kegan Smith, Costume Supervisor
Lyn Hope, Wardrobe Mistress
John Goodwin, Press and Publicity

Leslie Bridgewater, Music Adviser
Pauline Grant, Choreographer

THE THEATRE ORCHESTRA

Harold Ingram, Director : Nicholas Roth, Leader